Especially for

....

From

....

Date

....

Quiet
Moments
with God
· JOURNAL ·

HELEN STEINER RICE

DAYMAKER™
An Imprint of Barbour Publishing, Inc.

ISBN 978-1-63058-727-7

Published by DayMaker, an imprint of Barbour Publishing, Inc., P.O. Box 719, Uhrichsville, Ohio 44683, www.barbourbooks.com

Our mission is to publish and distribute inspirational products offering exceptional value and biblical encouragement to the masses.

Member of the
Evangelical Christian
Publishers Association

Printed in China.

God's Goodness

Wait with a heart that is patient
For the goodness of God to prevail—
For never do prayers go unanswered
And His mercy and love never fail.

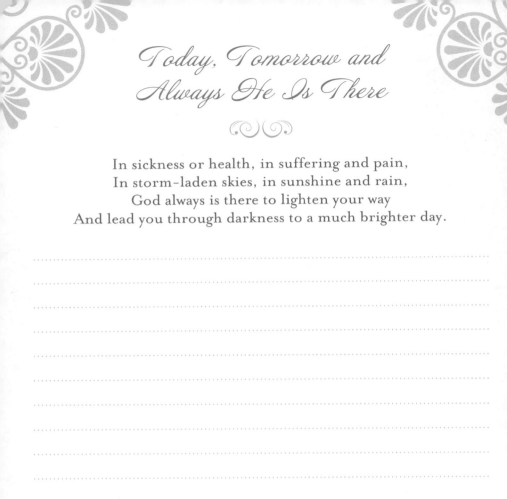

Today, Tomorrow and Always He Is There

In sickness or health, in suffering and pain,
In storm-laden skies, in sunshine and rain,
God always is there to lighten your way
And lead you through darkness to a much brighter day.

Channel of Blessing

Make me a channel of blessing today
I ask again and again when I pray.
Do I turn a deaf ear to the Master's voice
Or refuse to hear His direction and choice?
I only know at the end of the day
That I did so little to pay my way.

God's Promise

God has told us that nothing can sever
A life He created to live forever.
So let God's promise soften our sorrow
And give us new strength for a brighter tomorrow.

In His Footsteps

When we bring some pleasure to another human heart,
We have followed in His footsteps and we've had a little part
In serving God who loves us—for I'm very sure it's true
That in serving those around us, we serve and please God, too.

Now I Lay Me Down to Sleep

Into His hands each night as I sleep
I commend my soul for the dear Lord to keep,
Knowing that if my soul should take flight,
It will soar to the land where there is no night.

....
....
....
....
....
....
....
....
....
....
....
....
....
....
....
....
....

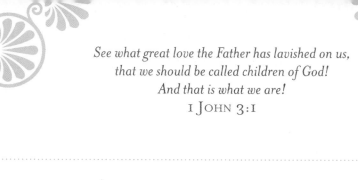

See what great love the Father has lavished on us,
that we should be called children of God!
And that is what we are!

1 JOHN 3:1

Heart Gifts

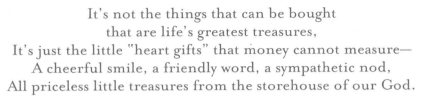

It's not the things that can be bought
that are life's greatest treasures,
It's just the little "heart gifts" that money cannot measure—
A cheerful smile, a friendly word, a sympathetic nod,
All priceless little treasures from the storehouse of our God.

....
....
....
....
....
....
....
....
....
....
....
....
....
....
....
....
....
....

Eternal Life

To know that life is endless
puts new purpose in our days
And fills our heart with joyous songs
of hope and love and praise.

God Is Never
Beyond Our Reach

God asks for no credentials—He accepts us with our flaws.
He is kind and understanding, and He welcomes us because
We are His erring children and He loves us, every one,
And He freely and completely forgives all that we have done.

Make Your Day Bright
by Thinking Right

Instead of just idle supposing,
step forward to meet each new day,
Secure in the knowledge God's near you,
to lead you each step of the way.

The Blessings of Sharing

Only what we give away
enriches us from day to day,
For not in getting but in giving
is found the lasting joy of living,
For no one ever had a part
in sharing treasures of the heart
Who did not feel the impact of
the magic mystery of God's love.

Give Me the Contentment of Acceptance

Let me say no to flattery and praise
And quietly spend the rest of my days
Far from the greed and the speed of man,
Who has so distorted God's simple life plan,
And let me be great in the eyes of You, Lord,
For that is the richest, most priceless reward.

Let Your Wish
Become a Prayer

There's no problem too big and no question too small—
Just ask God in faith and He'll answer them all—
Not always at once, so be patient and wait,
For God never comes too soon or too late.

In Him We Live and Move and Have Our Being

Life's a mystery man can't understand.
The great Giver of life is holding our hand,
And safe in His care there is no need for seeing,
"For in Him we live and move and have our being."

Expectation! Anticipation! Realization!

If we open the door to let joy walk through
When we learn to expect the best and the most, too,
And believing we'll find a happy surprise
Makes reality out of a fancied surmise.

....

....

....

....

....

....

....

....

....

....

....

....

....

....

....

....

....

....

The path of the righteous is like the morning sun,
shining ever brighter till the full light of day.
PROVERBS 4:18

The Way of the Cross Leads to God

If you are searching to find the way
To life everlasting and eternal day,
With faith in your heart take the path that He trod,
For the way of the cross is the way to God.

....

....

....

....

....

....

....

....

....

....

....

....

....

....

....

....

....

....

Spiritual Strength

Life can't always be a song—
You have to have trouble to make you strong,
So whenever you are troubled and everything goes wrong,
It is just God working in you to make your spirit strong.

Joy and Peace

God gives us a power we so seldom employ
For we're so unaware it is filled with such joy.
The gift that God gives us is anticipation,
Which we can fulfill with sincere expectation,
For there's power in belief when we think we will find
Joy for the heart and peace for the mind.

....
....
....
....
....
....
....
....
....
....
....
....
....
....

Flowers Leave Their Fragrance on the Hand that Bestows Them

You can't do a kindness without a reward—
Not in silver or gold but in joy from the Lord.
You can't light a candle to show others the way
Without feeling the warmth of that bright little ray,
And you can't pluck a rose all fragrant with dew
Without part of its fragrance remaining with you.

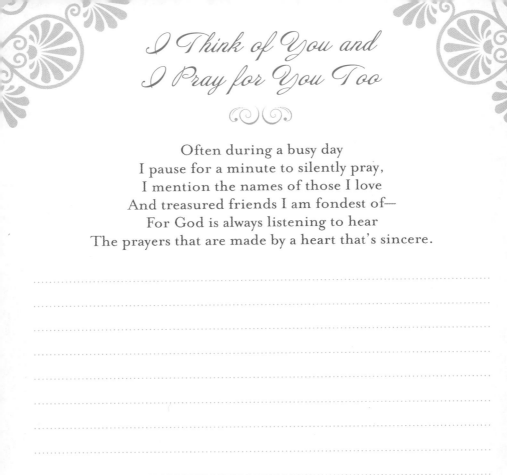

I Think of You and I Pray for You Too

Often during a busy day
I pause for a minute to silently pray,
I mention the names of those I love
And treasured friends I am fondest of—
For God is always listening to hear
The prayers that are made by a heart that's sincere.

Trust God in All Things

Take heart and meet each minute with faith in God's great love,
Aware that every day of life is controlled by God above. . . .
And never dread tomorrow or what the future brings—
Just pray for strength and courage and trust God in all things.

Somebody Cares

Somebody cares and always will—
The world forgets, but God loves you still.
You cannot go beyond His love
No matter what you're guilty of,
For God forgives until the end—
He is your faithful, loyal Friend.

Give Thanks Every Hour

We all have many things to be deeply thankful for,
But God's everlasting promise of life forevermore
Is a reason for thanksgiving every hour of the day
As we walk toward eternal life along the King's highway.

There Is Nothing New Under the Sun

There is nothing new beneath God's timeless sun,
And present, past, and future are all molded into one.
For the restless, unknown longing of my searching soul won't cease
Until God comes in glory and my soul at last finds peace.

But thanks be to God! He gives us the victory
through our Lord Jesus Christ.
1 CORINTHIANS 15:57

Showers of Blessings

No matter how big man's dreams are,
God's blessings are infinitely more,
For always God's giving is greater
than what man is asking for.

Thank You, God

Thank You, God, for the beauty around me everywhere,
The gentle rain and glistening dew, the sunshine and the air,
The joyous gift of feeling the soul's soft, whispering voice
That speaks to me from deep within and makes my heart rejoice.

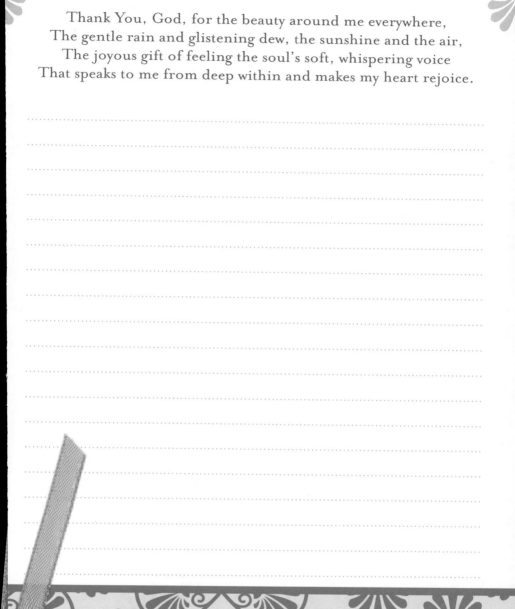

The Gift of Friendship

Friendship is a priceless gift
That can't be bought or sold,
And to have an understanding friend
Is worth far more than gold. . . .
And the golden chain of friendship is a strong and blessed tie
Binding kindred hearts together as the years go passing by.

A Child's Faith

Tiny hands and tousled heads
That kneel in prayer by little beds
Are closer to the dear Lord's heart
And of His kingdom more a part
Than we who search and never find
The answers to our questioning mind—
For faith in things we cannot see
Requires a child's simplicity.

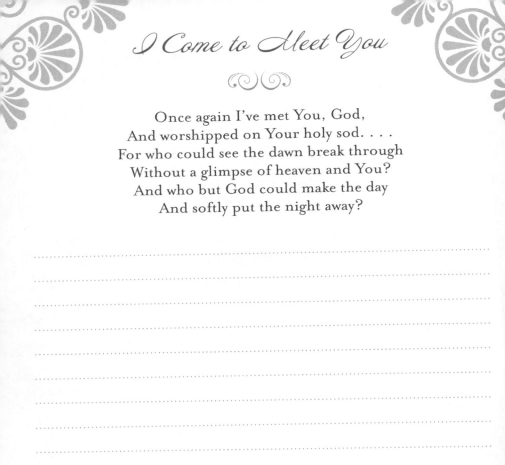

I Come to Meet You

Once again I've met You, God,
And worshipped on Your holy sod. . . .
For who could see the dawn break through
Without a glimpse of heaven and You?
And who but God could make the day
And softly put the night away?

A Prayer for the Young and Lovely

Oh teach me, dear God, to not rush ahead,
But to pray for Your guidance and to trust You instead. . . .
For You know what I need and that I'm only a slave
To the things that I want and desire and crave.

· ·
· ·
· ·
· ·
· ·
· ·
· ·
· ·
· ·
· ·
· ·
· ·
· ·
· ·
· ·
· ·
· ·

Guidance and Love

With God on your side, it matters not who
Is working to keep life's good things from you,
For you need nothing more than God's guidance and love
To ensure you the things that you're most worthy of.

The Magic of Love

Love is the language that every heart speaks,
For love is the one thing that every heart seeks. . . .
And where there is love God, too, will abide
And bless the family residing inside.

....

....

....

....

....

....

....

....

....

....

....

....

....

....

....

....

....

....

Showers of Blessings

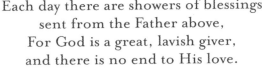

Each day there are showers of blessings
sent from the Father above,
For God is a great, lavish giver,
and there is no end to His love.

Dear friends, let us love one another,
for love comes from God.
Everyone who loves has been born
of God and knows God.
1 JOHN 4:7

My God Is No Stranger

How could I think God was far, far away
When I feel Him beside me every hour of the day?
And I've plenty of reasons to know God's my friend,
And this is one friendship that time cannot end.

Always Believe

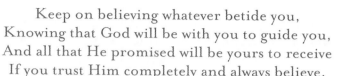

Keep on believing whatever betide you,
Knowing that God will be with you to guide you,
And all that He promised will be yours to receive
If you trust Him completely and always believe.

....
....
....
....
....
....
....
....
....
....
....
....
....
....
....
....
....
....
....

Good Morning, God!

You are ushering in another day, untouched and freshly new,
So here I am to ask You, God, if You'll renew me, too.
Forgive the many errors that I made yesterday
And let me try, dear God, to walk closer in Thy way.
But Father, I am well aware I can't make it on my own,
So take my hand and hold it tight for I can't walk alone.

Blessed

With faith in your heart, reach out for God's hand
And accept what He sends, though you can't understand. . . .
For our Father in heaven always knows what is best,
And if you trust His wisdom, your life will be blessed.

Life's Disappointments Are God's Sweetest Appointments

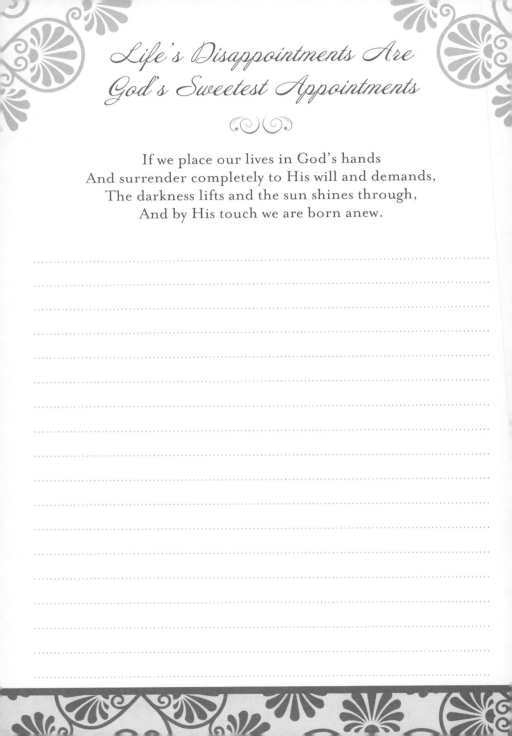

If we place our lives in God's hands
And surrender completely to His will and demands,
The darkness lifts and the sun shines through,
And by His touch we are born anew.

....
....
....
....
....
....
....
....
....
....
....
....
....
....
....
....
....
....
....
....
....

God's Nearness

The sky and the stars, the waves and the sea,
The dew on the grass, the leaves on a tree
Are constant reminders of God and His nearness
Proclaiming His presence with crystal-like clearness.

Wings of Love

The priceless gift of life is love,
For with the help of God above
Love can change the human race
And make this world a better place. . . .
For love dissolves all hate and fear
And makes our vision bright and clear
So we can see and rise above
Our pettiness on wings of love.

Higher Goal

Oh heavenly Father, grant again
A simple, childlike faith to men,
Forgetting color, race, and creed
And seeing only the heart's deep need.
For faith alone can save man's soul
And lead him to a higher goal.

Somebody Loves You

All of His treasures are yours to share
If you love Him completely and show that you care. . . .
And if you walk in His footsteps and have faith to believe,
There's nothing you ask for that you will not receive!

....
....
....
....
....
....
....
....
....
....
....
....
....
....
....
....
....
....
....
....

Truly my soul finds rest in God;
my salvation comes from him.
PSALM 62:1

Show Me

Show me the way to joy without end
With You as my Father, Redeemer, and Friend,
And send me the things that are hardest to bear,
And keep me forever safe in Thy care.

Climb till Your Dreams
Come True

Faith is a mover of mountains—
there's nothing that God cannot do—
So start out today with faith in your heart
and climb till your dream comes true.

"Love Divine, All Loves Excelling"

In a myriad of miraculous ways
God shapes our lives and changes our days.
Beyond our will or even knowing
God keeps our spirits ever growing.

God Is Our Encouragement

God has given us the answers which too often go unheeded,
But if we search His promises we'll find everything that's needed
To lift our faltering spirits and renew our courage, too,
For there's absolutely nothing too much for God to do.

Faith

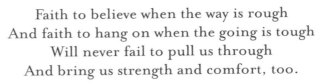

Faith to believe when the way is rough
And faith to hang on when the going is tough
Will never fail to pull us through
And bring us strength and comfort, too.

Be Glad

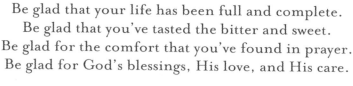

Be glad that your life has been full and complete.
Be glad that you've tasted the bitter and sweet.
Be glad for the comfort that you've found in prayer.
Be glad for God's blessings, His love, and His care.

....
....
....
....
....
....
....
....
....
....
....
....
....
....
....
....
....
....

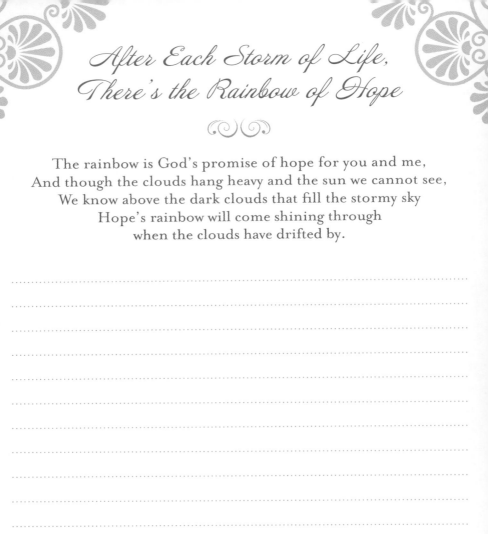

After Each Storm of Life, There's the Rainbow of Hope

The rainbow is God's promise of hope for you and me,
And though the clouds hang heavy and the sun we cannot see,
We know above the dark clouds that fill the stormy sky
Hope's rainbow will come shining through
when the clouds have drifted by.

Listen in the Quietness

When life becomes a problem much too great for us to bear,
Instead of trying to escape, let us withdraw in prayer—
For withdrawal means renewal if we withdraw to pray
And listen in the quietness to hear what God will say.

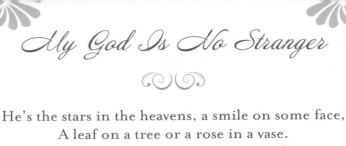

My God Is No Stranger

He's the stars in the heavens, a smile on some face,
A leaf on a tree or a rose in a vase.
He's winter and autumn and summer and spring—
In short, God is every real, wonderful thing.
I wish I might meet Him much more than I do—
I would if there were more people like you.

I know what it is to be in need, and I know what it is to have plenty. I have learned the secret of being content in any and every situation, whether well fed or hungry, whether living in plenty or in want. I can do all this through him who gives me strength.

PHILIPPIANS 4:12–13

Love One Another
As I Have Loved You

Love works in ways that are wondrous and strange,
And there is nothing in life that love cannot change,
And all that God promised will someday come true
When you have loved one another the way He loved you.

The House of Prayer

God only asks us to do our best—
Then He will take over and finish the rest. . . .
So when you are tired, discouraged, and blue,
There's always one door that is opened to you
And that is the door to the house of prayer,
And you'll find God waiting to meet you there.

Thank You, God, for Everything

Thank You, God, for everything—
the big things and the small—
For every good gift comes from God,
the giver of them all.

....
....
....
....
....
....
....
....
....
....
....
....
....
....
....
....

A Graduate's Prayer

Father, I have knowledge, so will You show me now
How to use it wisely and to find a way somehow
To make the world I live in a little better place
And to make life with its problems a bit easier to face?
Grant me faith and courage, and put purpose in my days,
And show me how to serve Thee in the most effective ways.

Talk It Over with God

There is only one place and only one Friend
Who is never too busy, and you can always depend
On Him to be waiting, with arms open wide
To hear all the troubles you came to confide. . . .
For the heavenly Father will always be there
When you seek Him and find Him at the altar of prayer.

Love One Another
As I Have Loved You

"Love one another, as I have loved you"
May seem impossible to do,
But if you will try to trust and believe,
Great are the joys that you will receive.

Forever Thanks

Give thanks for the blessings that daily are ours—
The warmth of the sun, the fragrance of flowers.
With thanks for all the thoughtful, caring things you always do
And a loving wish for happiness today and all year through!

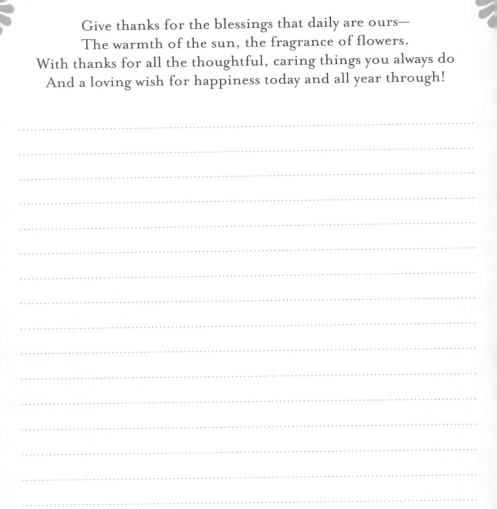

A Thankful Heart

Everyone needs someone to be thankful for,
And each day of life we are aware of this more,
For the joy of enjoying and the fullness of living
Are found only in hearts that are filled with thanksgiving.

After the Winter, God Sends the Spring

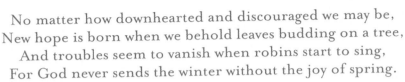

No matter how downhearted and discouraged we may be,
New hope is born when we behold leaves budding on a tree,
And troubles seem to vanish when robins start to sing,
For God never sends the winter without the joy of spring.

But the Lord is faithful, and he will strengthen
and protect you from the evil one. . . .
May the Lord direct your hearts into
God's love and Christ's perseverance.
2 THESSALONIANS 3:3, 5

....

....

....

....

....

....

....

....

....

....

....

....

....

....

....

....

....

....

....

....

....

....

....

....

God Loves Us

We are all God's children and He loves us, every one.
He freely and completely forgives all that we have done,
Asking only if we're ready to follow where He leads,
Content that in His wisdom He will answer all our needs.

Show Me the Way

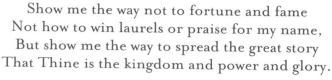

Show me the way not to fortune and fame
Not how to win laurels or praise for my name,
But show me the way to spread the great story
That Thine is the kingdom and power and glory.

Unaware, We Pass Him By

Hurrying along life's thoroughfare,
We passed Him by but remained unaware
That within the very sight of our eye,
Unnoticed, the Son of God passed by.

Childlike Faith

Only a child can completely accept
What probing adults research and reject.
O Father, grant once more to men
A simple, childlike faith again,
For only by faith and faith alone
Can we approach our Father's throne.

Daily Prayers Dissolve Your Cares

I meet God in the morning and go with Him through the day,
Then in the stillness of the night before sleep comes I pray
That God will just take over all the problems I couldn't solve,
And in the peacefulness of sleep my cares will all dissolve.

....
....
....
....
....
....
....
....
....
....
....
....
....
....
....
....
....

The Reflection of God

The silent stars in timeless skies,
The wonderment in children's eyes,
The autumn haze, the breath of spring,
The chirping song the crickets sing,
A rosebud in a slender vase
Are all reflections of God's face.

What Is Life?

Life is a sojourn here on earth
Which begins the day God gives us birth.
We enter this world from the great unknown,
And God gives each spirit a form of its own.

God So Loved the World

Our Father up in heaven, long, long years ago,
Looked down in His great mercy upon the earth below
And saw that folks were lonely and lost in deep despair,
And so He said, "I'll send My Son to walk among them there
So they can hear Him speaking and feel His nearness, too,
And see the many miracles that faith alone can do."

My Prayer

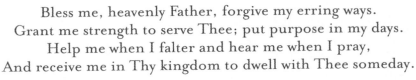

Bless me, heavenly Father, forgive my erring ways.
Grant me strength to serve Thee; put purpose in my days.
Help me when I falter and hear me when I pray,
And receive me in Thy kingdom to dwell with Thee someday.

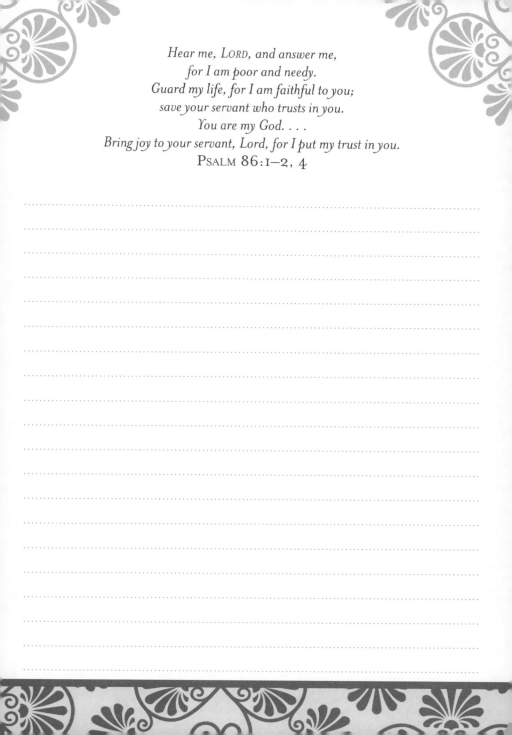

Hear me, LORD, and answer me,
for I am poor and needy.
Guard my life, for I am faithful to you;
save your servant who trusts in you.
You are my God. . . .
Bring joy to your servant, Lord, for I put my trust in you.
PSALM 86:1–2, 4

The Lord is our salvation and our strength in every fight,
Our Redeemer and Protector, our eternal guiding light.
He has promised to sustain us, He's our refuge from all harms,
And underneath this refuge are the everlasting arms.

Prayer for Renewal

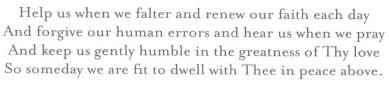

Help us when we falter and renew our faith each day
And forgive our human errors and hear us when we pray
And keep us gently humble in the greatness of Thy love
So someday we are fit to dwell with Thee in peace above.

....

....

....

....

....

....

....

....

....

....

....

....

....

....

....

....

....

....

Prayer for Guidance

As we pray for guidance, may a troubled world revive
Faith in God and confidence so our nation may survive,
And draw us ever closer to God and to each other
Until every stranger is a friend and every man a brother.

God Is Everywhere

Everywhere across the land
You see God's face and touch His hand
Each time you look up in the sky
Or watch the fluffy clouds drift by
Or touch a leaf or see a tree,
It's all God whispering "This is Me. . . .
And I am faith and I am light
And in Me there shall be no night."

Rich Satisfaction

May you find rich satisfaction
in your daily work and prayer,
And in knowing as you serve Him
He will keep you in His care.

God Will Not Fail You

When life seems empty and there's no place to go,
When your heart is troubled and your spirits are low,
When friends seem few and nobody cares—
There is always God to hear your prayers.

....

....

....

....

....

....

....

....

....

....

....

....

....

....

....

....

....

....

Come to Him

I cannot dwell apart from You—
You would not ask or want me to,
For You have room within Your heart
To make each child of Yours a part
Of You and all Your love and care
If we but come to You in prayer.

Meet Him

Meet Him in the morning and go with Him through the day
And thank Him for His guidance each evening when you pray—
And if you follow faithfully this daily way to pray,
You will never in your lifetime face another hopeless day.

....
....
....
....
....
....
....
....
....
....
....
....
....
....
....
....
....
....
....
....
....
....
....

Faith, Hope, Love

Hope to light our pathway when the way ahead is dark,
Hope to sing through stormy days with the sweetness of a lark,
Faith to trust in things unseen and know beyond all seeing
That it is in our Father's love we live and have our being,
And love to break down barriers of color, race, and creed,
Love to see and understand and help all those in need.

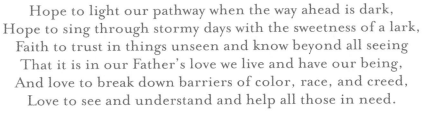

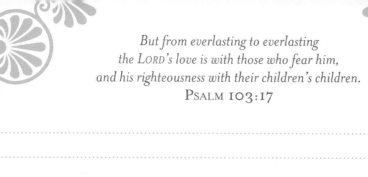

*But from everlasting to everlasting
the LORD's love is with those who fear him,
and his righteousness with their children's children.*

PSALM 103:17

Transforming Love

Love is enduring and patient and kind—
It judges all with the heart, not with the mind. . . .
And love can transform the most commonplace
Into beauty and splendor and sweetness and grace.

The House of Prayer

The house of prayer is no farther away
Than the quiet spot where you kneel and pray.
For the heart is a temple when God is there
As we place ourselves in His loving care.

....
....
....
....
....
....
....
....
....
....
....
....
....
....
....
....
....
....
....

Loving Thoughts

There's one rare and priceless gift that can't be sold or bought—
It's something poor or rich can give, for it's a loving thought. . . .
And loving thoughts are blessings for which no one can pay,
And only loving hearts can give this priceless gift away.

God's Assurance Gives Us Endurance

My blessings are so many, my troubles are so few—
How can I be discouraged when I know that I have You?
And I have the sweet assurance that there's nothing I need fear
If I but keep remembering I am Yours and You are near.

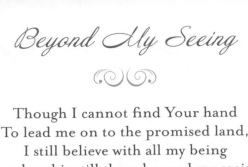

Beyond My Seeing

Though I cannot find Your hand
To lead me on to the promised land,
I still believe with all my being
Your hand is still there beyond my seeing.

....
....
....
....
....
....
....
....
....
....
....
....
....
....
....
....
....
....
....

What Is Love?

What is love? No words can define it—
It's something so great only God could design it.
Wonder of wonders, beyond man's conception—
And only in God can love find true perfection.

....
....
....
....
....
....
....
....
....
....
....
....
....
....
....
....
....
....
....

He Shares My Burden

Let me stop complaining about my load of care,
For God will always lighten it when it gets too much to bear. . . .
And if He does not ease my load, He'll give me strength to bear it,
For God, in love and mercy, is always near to share it.

Forever Yours

Kings and kingdoms all pass away—
nothing on earth endures. . . .
But the love of God who sent His Son
is forever and ever yours!

Mover of Mountains

Faith is a mover of mountains—
there's nothing man cannot achieve
If he has the courage to try it
and then has the faith to believe.

....

....

....

....

....

....

....

....

....

....

....

....

....

....

For ye shall go out with joy, and be led forth with peace:
the mountains and the hills shall break forth before you into singing,
and all the trees of the field shall clap their hands.
ISAIAH 55:12 KJV

He Loves You

It's amazing and incredible, but it's as true as it can be—
God loves and understands us all, and that means you and me.
His grace is all-sufficient for both the young and the old,
For the lonely and the timid, for the brash and for the bold.

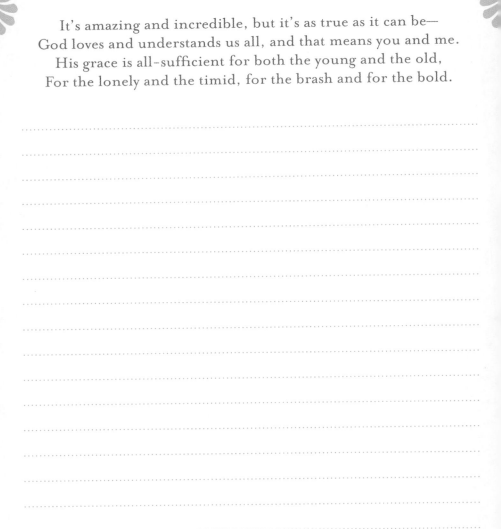

My Garden of Prayer

My garden beautifies my yard and adds fragrance to the air,
But it is also my cathedral and my quiet place of prayer.
So little do we realize that the glory and the power
Of Him who made the universe lies hidden in a flower.

Help from Above

God seems much closer and needed much more
When trouble and sorrow stand outside our door,
For then we seek shelter in His wondrous love,
And we ask Him to send us help from above.

Don't Give Up

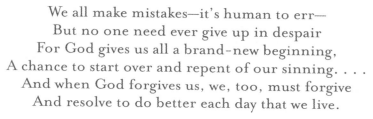

We all make mistakes—it's human to err—
But no one need ever give up in despair
For God gives us all a brand-new beginning,
A chance to start over and repent of our sinning. . . .
And when God forgives us, we, too, must forgive
And resolve to do better each day that we live.

What Is Prayer?

Prayer is much more than just asking for things—
It's the peace and contentment that quietness brings.
So thank You again for Your mercy and love
And for making me heir to Your kingdom above.

The Peace of Meditation

So we may know God better and feel His quiet power,
Let us daily keep in silence a meditation hour. . . .
For to understand God's greatness and to use His gifts each day,
The soul must learn to meet Him in a meditative way.

He Holds the Key

God in His goodness has promised
that the cross that He gives us to wear
Will never exceed our endurance
or be more Than our strength can bear. . . .
And secure in that blessed Assurance,
we can smile as we face tomorrow,
For God holds the key to the future
and no sorrow or care we need borrow.

God Loves Us Still

No matter what your past has been, trust God to understand.
And no matter what your problem is just place it in His hand—
For in all of our unloveliness this great God loves us still.
He loved us since the world began and what's more, He always will.

God Is Never
Beyond Our Reach

No one ever sought the Father and found He was not there,
And no burden is too heavy to be lightened by a prayer.
No problem is too intricate, and no sorrow that we face
Is too deep and devastating to be softened by His grace.

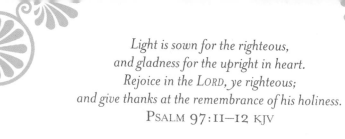

Light is sown for the righteous,
and gladness for the upright in heart.
Rejoice in the LORD, ye righteous;
and give thanks at the remembrance of his holiness.
PSALM 97:11–12 KJV

Wings of Prayer

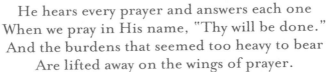

He hears every prayer and answers each one
When we pray in His name, "Thy will be done."
And the burdens that seemed too heavy to bear
Are lifted away on the wings of prayer.

What Is Love?

Love is unselfish, giving more than it takes—
And no matter what happens love never forsakes.
It's faithful and trusting and always believing,
Guileless and honest and never deceiving.
Yes, love is beyond what man can define,
For love is immortal and God's gift is divine!

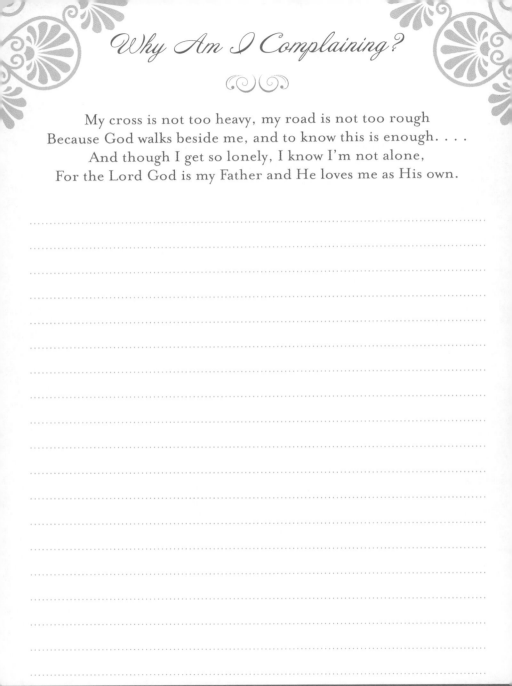

Why Am I Complaining?

My cross is not too heavy, my road is not too rough
Because God walks beside me, and to know this is enough. . . .
And though I get so lonely, I know I'm not alone,
For the Lord God is my Father and He loves me as His own.

Secure

When everything is quiet and we're lost in meditation
Our souls are then preparing for a deeper dedication
That will make it wholly possible to quietly endure
The violent world around us, for in God we are secure.

Strangers Are Friends We Haven't Met

God knows no strangers, He loves us all,
The poor, the rich, the great, the small.
He is a Friend who is always there
To share our troubles and lessen our care.

....
....
....
....
....
....
....
....
....
....
....
....
....
....
....
....
....
....

Never Alone

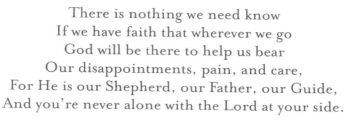

There is nothing we need know
If we have faith that wherever we go
God will be there to help us bear
Our disappointments, pain, and care,
For He is our Shepherd, our Father, our Guide,
And you're never alone with the Lord at your side.

· ·

· ·

· ·

· ·

· ·

· ·

· ·

· ·

· ·

· ·

· ·

· ·

· ·

· ·

· ·

Quiet Communion

Kneel in prayer in His presence
And you'll find no need to speak,
For softly in quiet communion,
God grants you the peace that you seek.

Creative Hand

In the beauty of a snowflake falling softly on the land
Is the mystery and the miracle of God's great, creative hand.
What better answers are there to prove His holy being
Than the wonders all around us that are ours just for the seeing?

Lose Yourself in Others

Open up your hardened heart and let God enter in,
He only wants to help you a new life to begin,
And every day's a good day to lose yourself in others,
And any time's a good time to see mankind as brothers,
And this can only happen when you realize it's true
That everyone needs someone and that someone is you.

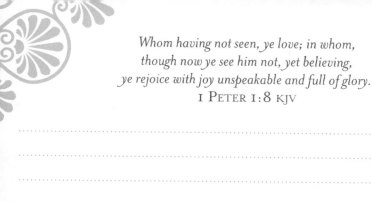

Whom having not seen, ye love; in whom,
though now ye see him not, yet believing,
ye rejoice with joy unspeakable and full of glory.
1 PETER 1:8 KJV

We Never Walk Alone

What more can we ask of our Father
than to know we are never alone,
That His mercy and love are unfailing
and He makes all our problems His own.

....
....
....
....
....
....
....
....
....
....
....
....
....
....
....
....

Help Once More

Thank God for the good things He has already done,
And be grateful to Him for the battles you've won—
And know that the same God who helped you before
Is ready and willing to help you once more.

....

....

....

....

....

....

....

....

....

....

....

....

....

....

....

....

....

....

....

....

Secure in His Love

Just close your eyes and open your heart
And feel your cares and worries depart.
Just yield yourself to the Father above
And let Him hold you secure in His love.

....
....
....
....
....
....
....
....
....
....
....
....
....
....
....
....
....

I Come to Meet You

I come to meet You, God, and as I linger here
I seem to feel You very near.
A rustling leaf, a rolling slope
Speak to my heart of endless hope.
The sun just rising in the sky,
The waking birdlings as they fly,
The grass all wet with morning dew
Are telling me I just met You.

My Daily Prayer

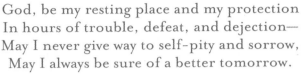

God, be my resting place and my protection
In hours of trouble, defeat, and dejection—
May I never give way to self-pity and sorrow,
May I always be sure of a better tomorrow.

....
....
....
....
....
....
....
....
....
....
....
....
....
....
....
....
....

Somebody Cares

He's ever-present and always there
To take you in His tender care
And bind the wounds and mend the breaks
When all the world around forsakes.
Somebody cares and loves you still,
And God is the Someone who always will.

Finding Faith in a Flower

Sometimes when faith is running low
And I cannot fathom why things are so,
I walk among the flowers that grow
And learn the answers to all I would know. . . .
And standing in silence and reverie,
My faith comes flooding back to me.

On the Wings of Prayer

On the wings of prayer our burdens take flight
And our load of care becomes bearably light
And our heavy hearts are lifted above
To be healed by the balm of God's wonderful love.

God's Love

God's love is like a sanctuary where our souls can find sweet rest
From the struggle and the tension of life's fast and futile quest.
God's love is like a tower rising far above the crowd,
And God's smile is like the sunshine
breaking through the threatening cloud.

For our heart shall rejoice in him,
because we have trusted in his holy name.
PSALM 33:21 KJV

He Lives

God lives in the beauty that comes with spring—
The colorful flower, the birds that sing—
And He lives in people as kind as you,
And He lives in all the nice things you do.

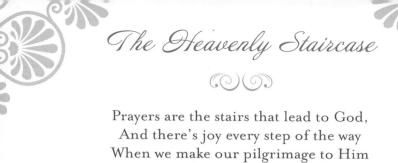

The Heavenly Staircase

Prayers are the stairs that lead to God,
And there's joy every step of the way
When we make our pilgrimage to Him
With love in our hearts each day.

God's Presence Is Ever Beside You

God's presence is ever beside you
as near as the reach of your hand.
You have but to tell Him your troubles—
there is nothing He won't understand.

....

....

....

....

....

....

....

....

....

....

....

....

....

....

....

....

....

Beyond Our Asking

More than hearts can imagine
or minds comprehend,
God's bountiful gifts
are ours without end.

Filled to the Brim

God has a storehouse
just filled to the brim
With all that man needs,
if we'll only ask Him.

....

....

....

....

....

....

....

....

....

....

....

....

....

....

....

....

....

Enfolded in His Love

The love of God surrounds us
Like the air we breathe around us,
As near as a heartbeat, as close as a prayer,
And whenever we need Him, He'll always be there.

....
....
....
....
....
....
....
....
....
....
....
....
....
....
....
....
....
....

Gifts from God

This brings you a million good wishes and more
For the things you cannot buy in a store—
Like faith to sustain you in times of trial,
A joy-filled heart and a happy smile,
Contentment, inner peace, and love—
All priceless gifts from God above!

Take Time to Be Kind

Kindness is a virtue given by the Lord.
It pays dividends in happiness, and joy is its reward,
For if you practice kindness in all you say and do,
The Lord will wrap His kindness all around your heart and you,
And wrapped within His kindness you are sheltered and secure,
And under His direction your way is safe and sure.

Blessings Devised
by God

God speaks to us in many ways,
Altering our lives, our plans, our days,
And His blessings come in many guises
That He alone in love devises.

Thou wilt shew me the path of life:
in thy presence is fulness of joy.
PSALM 16:11 KJV

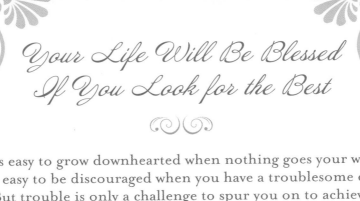

Your Life Will Be Blessed If You Look for the Best

It's easy to grow downhearted when nothing goes your way,
It's easy to be discouraged when you have a troublesome day,
But trouble is only a challenge to spur you on to achieve
The best that God has to offer if you have the faith to believe!

....
....
....
....
....
....
....
....
....
....
....
....
....
....
....
....
....

God Bless You
and Keep You

All who have God's blessing
can rest safely in His care,
For He promises safe passage
on the wings of faith and prayer.

Be Glad

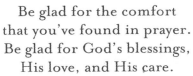

Be glad for the comfort
that you've found in prayer.
Be glad for God's blessings,
His love, and His care.

God's Keeping

To be in God's keeping is surely a blessing,
For though life is often dark and distressing,
No day is too dark and no burden too great
That God in His love cannot penetrate.

God's Love

God's love is like an island
in life's ocean, vast and wide,
A peaceful, quiet shelter
from the restless, rising tide.

Endless and Unfailing

God's love is like a beacon
burning bright with faith and prayer,
And through the changing scenes of life
we can find a haven there.

....
....
....
....
....
....
....
....
....
....
....
....
....
....
....
....
....
....
....
....
....
....

In God We Trust

It's easy to say "In God we trust"
when life's radiant and fair,
But the test of faith is only found
when there are burdens to bear.

Put Your Problems
In God's Hands

Although it sometimes seems to us our prayers have not been heard,
God always knows our every need without a single word,
And He will not forsake us even though the way is steep,
For always He is near us, a tender watch to keep.

Somebody Loves You

Somebody loves you more than you know
Somebody goes with you wherever you go. . . .
Don't think for a minute that this is not true,
For God loves His children and takes care of them, too.

Teach me to do your will,
for you are my God;
may your good Spirit
lead me on level ground.
PSALM 143:10

Begin Each Day by Kneeling to Pray

Start every day with a "good morning" prayer
And God will bless each thing you do and keep you in His care. . . .
And never, never sever the spirit's silken strand
That our Father up in heaven holds in His mighty hand.

Take Them to Him

The tears in our eyes are dried by the hands
of a loving Father who understands
All of our problems, our fears and despair
when we take them to Him on the wings of prayer.

The Key

As the heart opens, the dear Lord comes in,
And the prayer that we felt we could never begin
Is so easy to say, for the Lord understands
And He gives us new strength by the touch of His hands.

The Mystery of Prayer

There is nothing man can conceal that God does not already know. . . .
So kneel in His presence and you'll find no need to speak,
God grants you the peace that you seek.

Power of Prayer

I am only a worker employed by the Lord,
And great is my gladness and rich my reward
If I can just spread the wonderful story
That God is the answer to eternal glory.

Inspiration! Meditation!

Brighten your day and lighten your way
And lessen your cares with daily prayers.
Quiet your mind and leave tension behind
And find inspiration in hushed meditation.

The Hand of God

Accept what the year brings,
Seeing the hand of God in all things,
And as you grow in strength and grace,
The clearer you can see God's face.

In His Loving Care

May He who hears our every prayer
Keep you in His loving care—
And may you feel His presence near
Each day throughout the coming year.

Let Your Wish Become a Prayer

Put your dearest wish in God's hands today
And discuss it with Him as you faithfully pray,
And you can be sure your wish will come true
If God feels that your wish will be good for you.

Speaking to yourselves in psalms and hymns and spiritual songs,
singing and making melody in your heart to the Lord.
EPHESIANS 5:19 KJV

The Magic of Love

Love works in ways that are wondrous and strange,
And there is nothing in life that love cannot change,
And all that God promised will someday come true
When you love one another the way He loved you.

....
....
....
....
....
....
....
....
....
....
....
....
....
....
....
....
....
....
....

Infinitely More

No matter how big man's dreams are,
God's blessings are infinitely more,
For always God's giving is greater
than what man is asking for.

Forever True

When God makes a promise,
It remains forever true,
For everything God promises,
He unalterably will do.

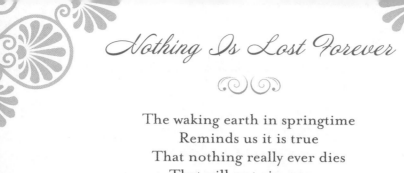

Nothing Is Lost Forever

The waking earth in springtime
Reminds us it is true
That nothing really ever dies
That will not rise anew.

....

....

....

....

....

....

....

....

....

....

....

....

....

....

....

....

....

....

....

....

Your Heart's Door

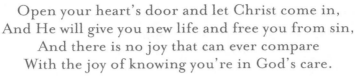

Open your heart's door and let Christ come in,
And He will give you new life and free you from sin,
And there is no joy that can ever compare
With the joy of knowing you're in God's care.

In Him We Live

Though we grow discouraged
In this world we're living in,
There is comfort just in knowing
God has triumphed over sin.
For our Savior's Resurrection
Was God's way of telling men
That in Christ we are eternal
And in Him we live again.

On Life's Busy Thoroughfares, We Meet with Angels Unawares

The unexpected kindness from an unexpected place,
A hand outstretched in friendship, a smile on someone's face,
A word of understanding spoken in an hour of trial
Are unexpected miracles that make life more worthwhile.

Only the Heart

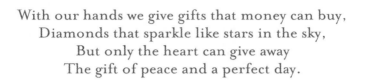

With our hands we give gifts that money can buy,
Diamonds that sparkle like stars in the sky,
But only the heart can give away
The gift of peace and a perfect day.

The Good Shepherd

[God's] goodness is unfailing, His kindness knows no end,
The Lord is a Good Shepherd on whom you can depend.
So when your heart is troubled, you'll find quiet, peace, and calm
If you'll open up the Bible and just read this treasured psalm.

Let the word of Christ dwell in you richly in all wisdom.
COLOSSIANS 3:16 KJV

A Bright World

A warm, ready smile or a kind, thoughtful deed
Or a hand outstretched in an hour of need
Can change our outlook and make the world bright
Where a minute before just nothing seemed right.

New Beginnings

It doesn't take a new year to begin our lives anew—
God grants us new beginnings each day the whole year through,
So never be discouraged for there comes daily to all men
The chance to make another start and begin all over again!

A Patient Heart

Wait with a heart that is patient
for the goodness of God to prevail,
For never do our prayers go unanswered
and His mercy and love never fail.

There's Peace and Calm
In the 23rd Psalm

With the Lord as your Shepherd you have all that you need,
For if you follow in His footsteps wherever He may lead,
He will guard and guide and keep you in His loving, watchful care,
And when traveling in dark valleys, your Shepherd will be there.